Free Run Productions in associat
Management and Neil McPherso
presents

The world premiere

Jab

by James McDermott

First performance at the Finborough Theatre: Tuesday, 20 February 2024

Jab
by James McDermott

Cast in order of appearance
Anne   **Kacey Ainsworth**
Don   **Liam Tobin**

Anne and Don's home, the UK, 2020–2021.

The approximate running time is 70 minutes.

There will be no interval.

Director	**Scott Le Crass**
Set and Costume Designer	**Leah Kelly**
Lighting Designer	**Jodie Underwood**
Composer	**Adam Langston**
Assistant Producer	**Kevin Nolan**
Associate Producer	**Sue Pomroy**
Assistant Director	**Josephine Rattigan**
Stage Manager	**Roel Fox**

Please see front of house notices or ask an usher for an exact running time.

Face masks are optional, except on Covid Safe Sunday matinees when they are mandatory.

Please turn your mobile phones off – the light they emit can be distracting.

Our patrons are respectfully reminded that, in this intimate theatre, any noise such as the rustling of programmes, talking or the ringing of mobile phones may distract the actors and your fellow audience members.

We regret there is no admittance or re-admittance to the auditorium whilst the performance is in progress.

Kacey Ainsworth | Anne

Trained at Royal Central School of Speech and Drama.

Theatre includes *Leaves of Glass* (Park Theatre), *Lava* (Soho Theatre), *Mam I'm Ere* (Royal Court Theatre, Liverpool), *Sweeney Todd* (Everyman Theatre, Liverpool), *Holes* (Nottingham Playhouse), *Feed the Beast* (Birmingham Rep, New Wolsey Theatre, Ipswich and Stephen Joseph Theatre, Scarborough), *Calendar Girls* (UK Tour), *Steel Magnolias* (UK Tour), *Carrie's War* (Apollo Theatre), *Sleep With Me* (National Theatre), *Serving It Up* (Bush Theatre) and *Pale Horse* and *Attempts on Her Life* (Royal Court Theatre).

Film includes *Lynne and Lucy, Mother, We the Kings, Hip Hip Hooray, Girl From Rio* and *Topsy Turvy*.

Television includes *Grantchester, Sliced, Moving On, The Worst Witch, Call the Midwife, Casualty, The Wright Way, Midsomer Murders, The Moonstone, Rock Chips, Holby Blue, Hotel Babylon, EastEnders, The Beggar Bride* and *The Accused*.

Radio includes *Torchwood* and *Doctor Who*.

Liam Tobin | Don

Theatre includes *Sweeney Todd* (Everyman Theatre, Liverpool), *Lights On Lights Off* (Shakespeare North Playhouse), *The Scousetrap, Mam I'm 'Ere!* (Royal Court Theatre, Liverpool), *HomeBaked* (Red Ladder and Royal Court Theatre, Liverpool), *Miracle On 34th Street* (Liverpool Playhouse), *Paint Your Wagon, A Clockwork Orange, The Big I Am, Fiddler On The Roof, Conquest of the South Pole, The Sum, Romeo and Juliet* (Liverpool Everyman Rep Company), *Benny* (Gilded Balloon at the Edinburgh Fringe), *The Hobbit* (Dukes Theatre, Lancaster), *Hamlet* (Theatr Clwyd), *Clybourne Park, When the Rain Stops Falling* (Unity Theatre, Liverpool), *A View From The Bridge* (Liverpool Playhouse), *One Flew Over The Cuckoo's Nest, Brief Encounter, Neville's Island, Dead Funny* (Torch Theatre, Milford Haven), *A Midsummer Night's Dream* and *She Stoops To Conquer* (Torch Theatre, Milford Haven and Mappa Mundi), *Cider With Rosie* and *The Merchant of Venice* (Theatre Royal Bury St. Edmunds), *Hoof!* (Hothouse Theatre, Los Angeles), *Gods Official* (West Yorkshire Playhouse) and *Pygmalion* (European Tour for the American Drama Group).

Film includes *Al's Lads*.

Television includes *Then and Now, Hollyoaks, Emmerdale, Coronation Street, The Royal, Heartbeat, The Cops, Seeing Red* and *The Second Coming*.

James McDermott | Playwright

Trained at the University of East Anglia with an MA (Distinction) in Scriptwriting, the Royal Court Writers Group, Soho Theatre's Writers Lab, Hampstead Theatre's Inspire: The Next Playwright Programme, Criterion Theatre's New Writing Programme and Menagerie Theatre's Young Writers Programme.

James's plays published by Concord Theatricals include *Time & Tide* which was nominated for an OffWestEnd Award for Best New Play and longlisted for the Bruntwood and Verity Bargate Awards (Park Theatre and East of England Tour) and *Rubber Ring*, winner of Pulse Festival's Suitcase Prize (Pleasance London and UK Tour). His other plays include *Acid's Reign* (VAULT Festival), *The Birds and The Bees* (New Wolsey Theatre, Ipswich and East of England Tour), *Shanty* (Sheringham Little Theatre), *Ghosted* (St George's Theatre, Great Yarmouth and Out There Festival) and *Robin Good: The Politico-Panto* (Norwich Playhouse). He has also written plays for BBC Radio 4 and is one of the writers on *EastEnders*.

James's poetry collections include *Wild Life*, shortlisted for The East Anglian Book Awards (Nine Arches Press), *Erased* (Polari Press) and *Manatomy*, longlisted for Polari's First Book Prize (Burning Eye Books). James is an Arvon writing tutor, teaches playwriting for the National Theatre's New Views schools programme and lectures in creative writing at the University of East Anglia.

Scott Le Crass | Director

Scott was born in Bristol, grew up in Birmingham, trained as an actor at Arts Ed and was a director on the Birmingham Rep's first Foundry Programme. In 2022, he completed the National Theatre Director's Course.

Scott directed the OffComm award winning digital revival of *Rose* by Martin Sherman, starring Maureen Lipman, winner of the OffWestEnd Award for Best Solo Performance (Hope Mill Theatre, Manchester, Sky Arts and Broadway HD and Ambassadors Theatre). For *Rose*, he was nominated for Best Creative West End Debut at The Stage Awards and was nominated for an OffWestEnd and Broadway World nomination for Best Director.

Direction includes *Cut The Crap* starring Sharon Osbourne (Fortune Theatre), *Toxic* (HOME, Manchester), *Buff* (Edinburgh Fringe and Plymouth Theatre Royal), *Seance* (UK Tour), *The Railway Children* (OVO Roman Theatre), *My Dear Aunty Nell* (Tour), *Behold! The Monkey Jesus* (Brockley Jack Studio Theatre), *Self Tape* (King's Head Theatre), *Merboy* (Omnibus Theatre), *Buff, Thirsty* (Vault Festival), *Twelfth Night* (East London Shakespeare Festival), *I Couldn't Do Your Job* (Pleasance London and Queens Theatre, Hornchurch), *Elmer* (UK and International

Tour for Sell A Door), *Sid* (Arts Theatre and UK Tour), *Country Music* (Omnibus Theatre), *The Witches* (Watford Palace Theatre), *Alice in Wonderland* (Old Rep, Birmingham), *If You Love Me This Might Hurt* by Matty May (Camden People's Theatre), *Education, Education Karaoke* (Camden People's Theatre), *Darling* (Hope Theatre), *Rage, But Hope* (Streatham Space Project), *The Chechnya Plays* (King's Head Theatre and Theatre Deli), *Kicked in the Sh**ter* (Hope Theatre and Theatre in The Mill, Bradford), *Cancel The Sunshine* (Hope Theatre), *The Killing of Sister George* (London Theatre Workshop), *Open House* (Birmingham Rep and Midlands Tour) and *Diary of a Madman* (Omnibus Theatre and Brockley Jack Studio Theatre).

Associate Direction includes *Godspell* (50th Anniversary Concert and Broadway HD) and *The Seven Ages of Patience* (Kiln Theatre).

Assistant Direction includes *The King's Speech* (Chichester Festival Theatre, Birmingham Rep and UK Tour), *Coming Up* (Watford Palace Theatre), *A Christmas Carol* (Birmingham Rep), *Von Ribbentrop's Watch* (Oxford Playhouse and Watford Palace Theatre), *Kurt and Sid* (Trafalgar Studios), *Romeo and Juliet*, *The Merchant of Venice* (Silvano Toti Globe) and *Dorian: A Rock Musical* (Ruby in the Dust and Stream Theatre).

He is an Associate Director for Pleasure Dome Theatre Company and has directed all of their productions to date including *A Christmas Carol* (Brewhouse, Taunton), *Rosalie* (Arlington Court and South West Tour), *Louisa* (South West Tour) and *A Midsummer Night's Dream* (The Valley of Rocks).

Leah Kelly | Set and Costume Designer
Trained in Fine Art at Manchester School of Art.
Leah is a visual artist based in London. This is her theatrical debut.

Jodie Underwood | Lighting Designer
Trained at RADA.
Lighting includes *A Christmas Carol* (Brewhouse Taunton), *Cheeky Little Brown* (UK Tour), *The Life Sporadic of Jess Wildgoose* (Pleasance London and Pleasance Edinburgh), *DNA* (Tara Theatre), *After The Act* (New Diorama Theatre and Traverse Theatre, Edinburgh), *Blow Down* (Theatre Royal Wakefield and Leeds Playhouse), *The Boys Are Kissing* (Theatre503) and *Horse-Play* (Riverside Studios).
Associate Lighting Designs include *Ruckus* (UK Tour), *The Book Of Will* (Shakespeare North Playhouse), *Ride* (Leicester Curve and Southwark Playhouse), *Pigs Might Fly* (Theatre Peckham) and *When Darkness Falls* (UK Tour).

Adam Langston | Composer

Adam has immersed himself in film music and songs since his childhood in Stroud on the edge of the Cotswolds. He worked extensively with director Tom Hooper and editor Melanie Oliver on *Cats*, creating arrangements and additional music in the cutting room (as well as playing rehearsal piano when needed). He also orchestrated Billie Eilish's song *No Time To Die* for Hans Zimmer, which won the Oscar for Best Original Song. Adam has been fortunate to work with Guy Chambers, including orchestrations for his folk musical *The Selfish Giant* (Vaudeville Theatre) and for Robbie Williams' no.1 album *The Christmas Present*.

Compositions include *Miss Willoughby and the Haunted Bookshop* (starring Kelsey Grammer), *Splinter* (starring Bill Fellows and Jane Asher), *Mia and the Dragon Princess* (starring Paul McGann). Orchestrations include *Les Misérables* (directed by Tom Hooper), *Alien: Covenant* (directed by Ridley Scott), *In the Heart of the Sea* (directed by Ron Howard), *White House Down* (directed by Roland Emmerich). Adam composed additional music for *In Bruges* (directed by Martin McDonagh), *Great Expectations* (directed by Mike Newell), *Walking With Dinosaurs* (worldwide arena Tour) and arranged ambient and orchestral music for *August: Osage County* (directed by John Wells). Animation work includes orchestral arrangements and production for Oscar-nominated animated films *Robin Robin* (Aardman) and *Revolting Rhymes* (Magic Light Pictures), Paramount Pictures' animated feature *The Little Prince* (directed by Mark Osborne) and *Frozen* arrangements for Walt Disney Resorts in Florida and Tokyo.

As well as scoring numerous feature films and shorts, Adam has composed for Harper's Bazaar and Vogue fashion editorials and an original musical for Royal Caribbean.

Other live work includes *Batman*, *Fast and Furious* and *Tomb Raider* arena tours. He has written songs with country pop star Twinnie and singer-songwriter Stacey Jackson. Adam enjoys writing music for charities, including Children in Need, the Special Olympics and the Military Wives Choirs, whose album *Remember* features his song *Carry Me*. He contributed music to the London 2012 Olympics Opening Ceremony and the Queen's Diamond Jubilee Concert at Buckingham Palace (for which he was Assistant Musical Director).

Adam was awarded Associateship of the Royal Academy of Music in 2019.

Sue Pomroy | Associate Producer

Sue is the Director of SJP Management, working in theatre and television as a director, theatrical agent and audition and acting coach. She trained actors and teachers worldwide for The Educational Drama Association. SJP Management has trained the UK WorldSkills competitors in confidence and presentation since 2010.

Kevin Nolan | Assistant Producer
Kevin was Producer for *Buff* by Ben Fensome (Edinburgh Festival) and
Associate Producer for *Country Music* (Omnibus Theatre).
He is co-founder of Queers & Thespians, a London-based LGBTQ+
community drama group, writing and co-producing the company's
first production, *A Queermas Carol*. During the COVID-19 pandemic,
he wrote and directed the company's two online productions *Queer
Shame* and *We 3 Queers*.

Josephine Rattigan | Assistant Director
Trained at Bristol Old Vic Theatre School.
Direction includes *Sunburn* (Old Red Lion Theatre) and Assistant
Direction at CYTO – Croydon Youth Theatre Company.
She is Artistic Director of Play In The Park playinthepark.co.uk

Roel Fox | Stage Manager
Stage Management includes *South Kentish Town* (Arcola Theatre),
Improbotics: Rosetta Stone (Rich Mix), *Pool No Water*, *Fury*, *4:48 Psychosis*,
Attempts On Her Life, *Playing With Grown-Ups*, *An Absolute Farce Of
A Murder Mystery*, *Love and Money*, *Roberto Zucco* (Drayton Arms
Theatre), *Don Juan Comes Back From The War* (New Diorama Theatre),
Wild East (Theatre503), *A Doll's House* (Teatro Technis), *Generation
WHYYY* (The Rose and Crown), *Crazy For Loving You* (Union Theatre), *A
Final Act Of Friendship* (White Bear Theatre and Bridge House Theatre),
Harry's Christmas, *One Man Poe* (King's Head Theatre), *Buff* (Vaults
Festival), *Behold! The Monkey Jesus* (Brockley Jack Studio Theatre) and
Love And Information (Chelsea Theatre).

FINBOROUGH THEATRE

"Probably the most influential fringe theatre in the world."
Time Out

"Under Neil McPherson, possibly the most unsung of all major artistic directors in Britain, the Finborough has continued to plough a fertile path of new plays and rare revivals that gives it an influence disproportionate to its tiny 50-seat size."
Mark Shenton, *The Stage*

"The mighty little Finborough which, under Neil McPherson, continues to offer a mixture of neglected classics and new writing in a cannily curated mix."
Lyn Gardner, *The Stage*

"The tiny but mighty Finborough"
Ben Brantley, *The New York Times*

Founded in 1980, the multi-award-winning Finborough Theatre presents plays and music theatre, concentrated exclusively on vibrant new writing and unique rediscoveries – both in our 1868 Victorian home and online with our digital initiative – #FinboroughFrontier

Our programme is unique – we never present work that has been seen anywhere in London during the last 25 years. Behind the scenes, we continue to discover and develop a new generation of theatre makers. Despite remaining completely unsubsidised, the Finborough Theatre has an unparalleled track record for attracting the finest talent who go on to become leading voices in British theatre. Under Artistic Director Neil McPherson, it has discovered some of the UK's most exciting new playwrights including Laura Wade, James Graham, Mike Bartlett, Jack Thorne, Carmen Nasr, Athena Stevens and Anders Lustgarten and directors including Tamara Harvey, Robert Hastie, Tom Littler, Blanche McIntyre, Kate Wasserberg and Sam Yates.

Artists working at the theatre in the 1980s included Clive Barker, Rory Bremner, Nica Burns, Kathy Burke, Ken Campbell, Jane Horrocks, Nicola Walker and Claire Dowie. In the 1990s, the Finborough Theatre first became known for new writing including Naomi Wallace's first play *The War Boys*, Rachel Weisz in David Farr's *Neville Southall's Washbag*, four plays by Anthony Neilson including *Penetrator* and *The Censor*, both of which transferred to the Royal Court Theatre and new plays by Richard Bean, Lucinda Coxon, David Eldridge and Tony Marchant. New writing development included the premieres of modern classics such as Mark Ravenhill's *Shopping and F***king*, Conor McPherson's *This Lime Tree Bower*, Naomi Wallace's *Slaughter City* and Martin McDonagh's *The Pillowman*.

Since 2000, new British plays have included Laura Wade's London debut *Young Emma* (commissioned by the Finborough Theatre), James Graham's London debut *Albert's Boy* with Victor Spinetti and four other of his first plays, Sarah Grochala's S27, Athena Stevens' *Schism* which was nominated for an Olivier Award, West End transfers for Joy Wilkinson's *Fair*, Nicholas de Jongh's *Plague Over England*, Jack Thorne's *Fanny and Faggot*, Neil McPherson's Olivier Award nominated *It Is Easy To Be Dead* and Dawn King's *Foxfinder* and a New York transfer for Sophie Swithinbank's *Bacon*.

UK premieres of foreign plays have included plays by Lanford Wilson, Larry Kramer, Tennessee Williams, Suzan-Lori Parks, the English premieres of two Scots language classics by Robert McLellan and more Canadian plays than any other theatre in Europe, with West End transfers for Frank McGuinness' *Gates of Gold* with William Gaunt, Craig Higginson's *Dream of the Dog* with Dame Janet Suzman and Jordan Tannahill's *Late Company*. In December 2022, the Finborough Theatre became the first foreign theatre to perform in Ukraine since the Russian invasion with *Pussycat in Memory of Darkness* which has subsequently revisited Kyiv and played in Germany and the USA.

Rediscoveries of neglected work – most commissioned by the Finborough Theatre – have included the first London revivals of Rolf Hochhuth's *Soldiers* and *The Representative*, both parts of Keith Dewhurst's *Lark Rise to Candleford*, *Etta Jenks* with Clarke Peters and Daniela Nardini, three rediscoveries from Noël Coward, Terence Rattigan's *Variation On A Theme* with Rachael Stirling and Lennox Robinson's *Drama at Inish* with Celia Imrie and Paul O'Grady. Transfers have included Emlyn Williams' *Accolade*, John Van Druten's *London Wall* and J. B. Priestley's *Cornelius* which had a sell-out Off-Broadway run in New York City.

Music Theatre has included the new and the old, including the acclaimed 'Celebrating British Music Theatre' series, with West End transfers for Adam Gwon's *Ordinary Days* and the UK premiere of Rodgers and Hammerstein's *State Fair*. Specially curated playlists of Finborough Theatre music theatre are available to listen to for free on Spotify.

The Finborough Theatre won the 2020 and 2022 London Pub Theatres Pub Theatre of the Year Award, The Stage Fringe Theatre of the Year Award in 2011, the Empty Space Peter Brook Award in 2010 and 2012 and nominated in 2023 and was nominated for an Olivier Award in 2017 and 2019. Artistic Director Neil McPherson was awarded the Critics' Circle Special Award for Services to Theatre in 2019. It is the only unsubsidised theatre ever to be awarded the Channel 4 Playwrights Scheme bursary twelve times.

www.finboroughtheatre.co.uk

FINBOROUGH THEATRE

The Finborough Theatre is a member of the Independent Theatre Council, the Society of Independent Theatres, Musical Theatre Network, The Friends of Brompton Cemetery, The Earl's Court Society, The Kensington Society and the WEST Theatre Association, Kyiv, Ukraine.

Supported by
The Carne Trust
The Earls Court Development Company
Theatres Trust

Supported by players of
People's Postcode Lottery

Awarded funds from
Postcode Society Trust

The Finborough Theatre has the support of the Peggy Ramsay Foundation / Film 4 Playwrights Awards Scheme.

Mailing
Email admin@finboroughtheatre.co.uk or give your details to our Box Office staff to join our free email list.

Playscripts
Many of the Finborough Theatre's plays have been published and are on sale from our website.

Environment
The Finborough Theatre has a 100% sustainable electricity supply.

Local History
The Finborough Theatre's local history website is online at www. earlscourtlocalhistory.co.uk

The Finborough Theatre on Social Media
www.facebook.com/FinboroughTheatre
www.twitter.com/finborough
www.instagram.com/finboroughtheatre
www.youtube.com/user/finboroughtheatre
www.tiktok.com/@finboroughtheatre
www.threads.net/@finboroughtheatre
Search 'Finborough Theatre' on Spotify for specially curated playlists

Friends of the Finborough Theatre
The Finborough Theatre is a registered charity. We receive no public funding and rely solely on the support of our audiences.
Please do consider supporting us by joining our newly relaunched Friends of the Finborough Theatre scheme.

There are five categories of Friends, each offering a wide range of benefits. Please ask any member of our staff for a leaflet.

William Terriss Friends – Anonymous. Catrin Evans. Anne and Patrick Foster. Janet and Leo Liebster. Ros and Alan Haigh.
Adelaide Neilson Friends – Charles Glanville. Philip G Hooker.
Legacy Gifts – Tom Erhardt.

JAB

by James McDermott

∥SAMUEL FRENCH∥

FOR AMATEUR PRODUCTION ENQUIRIES

UNITED KINGDOM AND WORLD
EXCLUDING NORTH AMERICA
licensing@concordtheatricals.co.uk

020-7054-7298

Each title is subject to availability from Concord Theatricals,
depending upon country of performance.

USE OF COPYRIGHTED MUSIC

USE OF COPYRIGHTED THIRD-PARTY MATERIALS

IMPORTANT BILLING AND CREDIT REQUIREMENTS

This programme text is based on a rehearsal script, and may differ slightly from the play as performed.

CHARACTERS

ANNE – fifty eight, NHS worker.
DON – sixty, vintage shop keeper.

SETTING

Anne and Don's house, UK.

TIME

2020-2021

AUTHOR'S NOTES

This play is based on my NHS worker mother and anti-vaxxer father's declining relationship in lockdown. Until their relationship finally soured, my parents seemed to enjoy their constant boozy bickering. They'd often say things they didn't mean to amuse, shock or play with one another. It was familiar and strangely cosy to them. Perhaps this could be reflected in the production.

Jab *is inspired by the events that unfolded in my parents'*
relationship during the COVID-19 lockdowns.

This play is dedicated to my Mum and Dad.

One

*(To thumping eighties pop, maybe "Sweet Dreams" by the Eurythmics, **ANNE** and **DON** drunk dance together joyously, as if they've just met in a nightclub.)*

(They do this for some time, loving it, loving life, falling in love with each other.)

(Then, as the music gets louder, harder, faster, their dancing becomes more intense, sexualised, animal.)

(They dance like this for too long.)

*(Then two armchairs emerge from the darkness and grow clearer, nearer, trapping **ANNE** and **DON**, forcing them too close together.)*

*(And as the music and lights distort, suddenly it's hard to tell if **ANNE** and **DON** are dancing or fighting.)*

(They move like this for too long.)

(And then they push each other away.)

(And they fall down into their respective armchairs.)

(And instantly the music ends like a shock.)

Two

*(**ANNE** and **DON** in their respective armchairs, each drinking a glass of white wine, watching TV. A bottle of wine by each of their chairs. They enjoy their bickering.)*

ANNE. Can't believe what I'm watching.

DON. I can. Knew this would happen.

ANNE. Work said it could go on for three months…

DON. Bollocks could it.

ANNE. You don't know.

DON. Read it in paper.

ANNE. Hope the boys'll be alright.

DON. What you on about? They'll be fine.

ANNE. Suppose they're young, healthy…

DON. Just a bad cold.

ANNE. It's not.

DON. It is.

ANNE. I work on front line of it.

DON. Front line of it! You're behind a desk.

*(**DON** drinks.)*

ANNE. You'll have to shut shop.

DON. I know…

ANNE. Not that it makes money.

DON. Makes millions.

ANNE. Makes nothing.

DON. My head space that shop…

ANNE. A hobby, not a business. You can only afford to keep it 'cause I keep you.

(**DON** *drinks.*)

You can get a job.

DON. I can have a rest.

ANNE. Had a rest for twenty-nine years.

DON. Married to you?

ANNE. You will: you'll have to get a job.

DON. I've got a job.

ANNE. Sat in vintage shop? Reading paper? Drinking coffee chatting to Chris next door?

(**DON** *drinks.*)

Well you can't do that now.

DON. I know...

ANNE. You're non-essential.

DON. I'm what?

ANNE. Non-essential. You're non-essential.

DON. Like a luxury item. I'm a bath bomb.

ANNE. You can get a job at big Tesco.

DON. I can't...

ANNE. Why not?

DON. I'll...be open again in a month.

ANNE. You're not doing nothing for three months.

DON. Not be three months. And I not be doing nothing. Be sowing my seeds.

ANNE. You what?

DON. Doing my garden. And we can do stuff?

ANNE. I've got work to do.

DON. Not all the time.

ANNE. I'm not non-essential. So if I'm working, you're working.

DON. Well I'm not stacking shelves.

ANNE. Think you're too good for it?

DON. Shut up I can't hear this.

ANNE. Everyone else who's non-essential – they'll have to do it.

DON. I'm missing this.

ANNE. Tesco wouldn't want you anyway.

> (**DON** *turns up the TV with the remote.*)

Underqualified.

> (**DON** *turns the volume up on the TV with the remote.*)

No people skills.

> (**DON** *turns the volume louder on the TV with the remote.*)

And what with your back…

DON. Nothing wrong with my back.

ANNE. It's had it.

DON. In mint condition my back.

ANNE. Had it 'cause you're never off it: always snoring on that settee.

DON. Not me who's never off their back…

ANNE. You make me sick when you come out with stuff like that.

>   (**DON** *sniggers.*)

Degrading. Demeaning. Sexist.

DON. Not sexist. Give over woman. It's a joke.

ANNE. You're the joke.

DON. Here she goes.

ANNE. You're sixty.

DON. So?

ANNE. So stop banging on about sex all the time. Like living with Sid James.

>   (**DON** *does a bad impression of Sid James's laugh.*)

Who's that meant to be?

DON. You. After a drink.

ANNE. I'll be drinking if I'm stuck in with you.

DON. Not be stuck in.

ANNE. Caged like animals.

DON. We can have two walks a day.

ANNE. Imprisoned with you for three months...

>   (**ANNE** *drinks. Perhaps they share a smirk, enjoying their age-old boozy banter.*)

DON. Not be three months: told you.

ANNE. Always locked in with you...

DON. You're always out.

ANNE. When? Where?

DON. With your friends.

ANNE. Not my fault you don't have any.

      (**DON** *drinks.*)

DON. You go out to do big shop. We go to car boots.

ANNE. To find vintage stock...

DON. There you go then. What more do you want?

ANNE. Go for dinner.

DON. Don't know who's cooked it.

ANNE. Go dancing.

DON. Two left feet.

ANNE. Not with you. With the girls.

DON. They're sixty.

ANNE. Go abroad.

DON. Wouldn't get me on a plane.

ANNE. Or a boat, a train...

DON. Happy at home. Happy with you.

ANNE. Get you up a ladder though: if we're stuck in, you can do the house.

DON. House don't need doing.

ANNE. Living room does. Look at it.

DON. It's fine.

ANNE. Peeling walls. Damp on corner of that roof.

DON. It's fine woman.

ANNE. You're doing it. Only reason I don't divorce you: you can decorate. I want it done.

      (**ANNE** *drinks.*)

DON. Natural Calico?

ANNE. What?

DON. Or Natural Hessian?

ANNE. Whatever colour the walls are now...

DON. I don't know. You paid for the paint. You pay for everything. So what colour is this on the Dulux colour chart?

> (**ANNE** *drinks.*)

Dusted Fondant? Buttermilk? White Mist? Magnolia? Goose Down?

> (*They smirk at each other, enjoying the game.*)

ANNE. Goose Down.

DON. Don't look like Goose Down to me...

ANNE. I said it's Goose Down.

DON. It's Magnolia.

ANNE. Well I want it painting Goose Down.

DON. Good job. 'Cause that's what it is. Not that we can get paint: shops are shut.

> (**DON** *drinks and burps slightly.*)

ANNE. Least I won't have to see you all the time. I'll be too busy working from home.

DON. I can't make noise doing the house then. Not with my back.

> (**DON** *drinks.*)

> (**ANNE** *drinks.*)

Fifty dead...

> (**ANNE** *stares at* **DON** *who stares out at the TV.*)

> (*They drink.*)

Three

(**ANNE** *and* **DON** *sit in their armchairs in front of the TV.*)

(**ANNE** *does work emails on her phone.*)

(**DON** *watches TV.*)

(*They drink their white wine.*)

(**DON** *belches.*)

(**ANNE** *glares at* **DON** *who stares at the TV.*)

(*Time passes.*)

(*They drink their white wine.*)

(**ANNE** *farts.*)

(**DON** *looks to* **ANNE** *who stares at her phone.*)

(*Time passes.*)

Four

(**ANNE** *and* **DON** *sit in their armchairs watching TV.*)

ANNE. *The Durrells.*

DON. *Emmerdale.*

ANNE. You had *Emmerdale* last night.

DON. Having it tonight.

ANNE. Every night for a fortnight.

DON. It's tradition.

ANNE. It's torture. Put *The Durrells* on.

DON. Not watching that shit.

ANNE. But I have to watch this shit?

DON. You only watch 'Durrells' for her clothes.

ANNE. They're vintage.

DON. Kelly Whats It.

ANNE. Keeley. Keeley Hawes. Pass me the box.

DON. Shut up it's on.

ANNE. Gimme the box.

DON. You're not changing it.

ANNE. Give me the bastard box.

DON. You're not. Fucking. Changing it.

ANNE. I pay the licence fee. Gimme the twatting cunting box.

(**DON** *picks up the remote but won't hand it to* **ANNE**.)

(**ANNE** *reaches for it but* **DON** *moves it away from her grasp.*)

(**ANNE** *grabs the TV remote from him and changes the channel to* The Durrells.)

(*They watch TV.*)

(**DON** *doo doo doo doo's a snatch of the* Emmerdale *theme loudly.*)

(**ANNE** *watches her programme.*)

(**DON** *removes a packet of cheese and onion crisps he's been sat on.*)

(**DON** *opens the crisps packet loudly.*)

(**ANNE** *watches her programme.*)

(**DON** *eats the whole bag of crisps slowly and loudly.*)

(**ANNE** *watches her programme.*)

(**DON** *noisily tips the crisps crumbs from the packet into his mouth.*)

(**ANNE** *watches her programme.*)

(**DON** *noisily folds the empty crisps packet into an origami triangle and pockets it.*)

(**ANNE** *watches her programme.*)

(**DON** *removes a second packet of cheese and onion crisps he's been sat on and opens them.*)

Nearly two hundred dead today...

Five

(**DON** *sits in his armchair watching TV.*)

(**ANNE** *enters.*)

ANNE. Boys are alright. Just text 'em.

DON. Say hello.

ANNE. I always do. Gammon's in.

DON. You covered it in pineapple?

ANNE. Yep.

DON. Hate it when you do that.

ANNE. I know.

DON. Least if I catch it, I'll lose my sense of taste…

ANNE. Thought you had already with that shirt…

DON. It's designer.

ANNE. Matalan's not designer. You'll need to watch gammon.

DON. Why will I?

ANNE. 'Cause I'm having a bath.

DON. I'm getting in.

ANNE. Not with me you're not.

DON. Don't wanna get in with you. I meant I'm getting in first.

ANNE. You never have a bath. Why you stink.

DON. Well I want one. So I'm getting in first.

ANNE. I've been at work all day.

DON. Sat talking at a laptop?

ANNE. Keeping you.

DON. I've been weeding.

ANNE. Weeding! I've been on meetings. With CCG.

DON. Weeding taraxacum officinale.

ANNE. Or Clinical Commissioning Group to you.

DON. Commonly known as dandelions.

ANNE. I know Monty Don.

DON. So I'm filthy. So I'm getting in bath first.

ANNE. You can get in after me. Not be long. Watch gammon.

DON. We'll toss for it.

ANNE. What?

>   (**DON** *removes a coin from his jeans pocket.*)

DON. Who gets in first.

ANNE. I pay water bill.

DON. Heads or tails?

>   (**ANNE** *stares at him.*)

Heads or tails?

ANNE. How've I stood a month of this?

DON. Heads.

>   (**DON** *tosses the coin, catches it on his hand,
>   looks at it.*)
>
>   (*A moment.*)

Don't use all hot water. And flick immersion on.

ANNE. Tosser.

(**ANNE** *glares at* **DON** *who returns to watching TV.*)

DON. Another five hundred dead today.

ANNE. Five hundred and one soon...

Six

*(ANNE sits in her armchair. DON stands by
the open door, which is unseen offstage.)*

ANNE. Shut that door.

DON. Who are you: Larry Grayson?

ANNE. I'm freezing.

DON. Not long now.

ANNE. Pointless.

DON. It's not.

ANNE. Insulting.

DON. It's grateful. All they're doing for the country. For
Bojo.

ANNE. If he's even got it. If they're that grateful, pay us
more.

DON. All about money with you.

ANNE. Would be with you if you had to earn it.

DON. Any minute now.

ANNE. You're only joining in to wind me up.

DON. Narcissist.

(Offstage, the distant sound of clapping.)

(DON joins in, clapping loudly.)

Joining in 'cause I'm grateful. For all you do.

ANNE. Sit down!

(DON claps louder.)

Sit. Down.

(A moment.)

*(***DON*** heads for his armchair...)*

*(Then **DON** reaches behind his armchair and picks up a pan and wooden spoon.)*

*(***ANNE*** laughs at his gall.)*

Don't you dare.

(A moment.)

*(Then **DON** starts beating the pan with the wooden spoon, loud as he can.)*

(A moment.)

*(And **ANNE** and **DON** burst out laughing.)*

Seven

(**ANNE** and **DON** *sit in their armchairs. They drink glasses of wine.*)

(*An empty wine bottle by each of their chairs.*)

(*From her phone,* **ANNE** *plays "Sweet Dreams" by the Eurythmics.*)

(**ANNE** *drunkenly sings the lyrics loudly.*)

(**DON** *drunkenly bobs his head along to the music.*)

ANNE. Playing when we met this…

DON. Chaser's Nightclub…

ANNE. Skegness…

DON. Skeggy!

ANNE. Skeggy Vegas!

DON. "Hello gorgeous" …

ANNE. "Hello lovely man" …

DON. Our song…

(**ANNE** *reaches for* **DON**'*s hand.*)

(*They hold hands.*)

ANNE. These hands…

DON. What about 'em?

ANNE. Held my boys. Held me when Dad died, Mum… our Tina…

(*A moment.*)

Twenty-nine years…

DON. Get less for murder...

> *(They laugh.)*

> *(**ANNE** drunkenly sings the lyrics loudly.)*

> *(**DON** drunkenly bobs his head along to the music.)*

> *(Then **ANNE** tugs on **DON**'s hand.)*

ANNE. Dance with me.

DON. Give over.

ANNE. Dance with me.

> *(They look at each other and smirk.)*

> *(**DON** tries to get up but groans with back pain.)*

> *(**ANNE** watches him as **DON** gives up.)*

DON. You're pissed woman.

> *(The music keeps playing.)*

> *(**ANNE** lets go of **DON**'s hand.)*

Over a thousand now...

> *(They both glug their wine.)*

Eight

(**ANNE** and **DON** sit in their armchairs watching TV.)

DON. Barnard Castle?

ANNE. Did you hear me?

DON. Test his bloody eyesight!

ANNE. Drafting us all in.

DON. Poke his pissing eyes out.

ANNE. Everyone. Everyone who works in NHS.

DON. Lock him up in a twatting castle...

ANNE. They want us to go out, look around abandoned buildings.

(**DON** watches TV.)

Old schools, office blocks, care homes: see if they're suitable...

(**DON** watches TV.)

So they can re-open 'em, turn 'em into hospitals...

(**DON** watches TV.)

Morgues...

(**DON** watches TV.)

Don.

DON. You what?

ANNE. I'll have to go out.

DON. Well don't go giving it to me.

(**ANNE** stares at **DON**.)

And if you're going out, we need crisps.

(A moment.)

ANNE. Don... I'm scared.

DON. It's your job.

*(**ANNE** glares at **DON** who stares at the TV.)*

Five thousand...

Nine

> (**ANNE** *and* **DON** *sit in their armchairs
> watching TV.*)

ANNE. How many times?

DON. I forgot.

ANNE. For twenty-nine years?

DON. Like you forgot crisps...

ANNE. Just put it down.

DON. You'd moan if I pissed on it.

ANNE. Lift it up to piss. Then put it down.

DON. You want putting down.

ANNE. And you didn't forget.

DON. I did.

ANNE. I know why you did it.

DON. Here she goes: Miss Marple.

ANNE. 'Cause of the shop.

DON. Shut up I'm missing this.

ANNE. Well it's going.

DON. It's not.

ANNE. I'm not renewing lease on shop that makes no
money.

> (**ANNE** *drinks.*)

DON. You can't.

ANNE. It's in my name: can do what I want.

> (*A moment.*)

DON. My head space that shop.

ANNE. What you need head space from? You don't have any stress.

DON. After three months of you?

ANNE. Need space from me, there's the door.

(*A moment.*)

DON. You'd miss me.

ANNE. I'd manage.

DON. Couldn't live without me.

ANNE. I'd live!

DON. Miss me when I'm gone.

ANNE. Be glad of the life insurance. And they'd be no twat leaving my toilet seat up.

(*A moment.*)

DON. Yeah well... I'm going nowhere.

ANNE. Story of your life. And I'm not keeping that shop. Told you this'd go on longer than three months: shop might never re-open.

DON. Give over.

ANNE. Get a proper job. Chris has. Keith. Sending me out in this, when you're sat in here safe and sound? I've had enough. Not keeping you any more.

(**ANNE** *drinks.*)

DON. Gimme fifty grand and I'll go.

(*A moment.*)

ANNE. What?

DON. Fifty grand. I'll go. Static caravan on Kelling Heath. Near the pub. The beach. My own toilet seat. To leave down and piss all over. That'll do me.

>   (**ANNE**, *surprised, looks at* **DON** *who watches TV. Is he bantering? Is he serious?*)

ANNE. Give you half? Of everything I've worked for? Wouldn't give you satisfaction.

>   (**ANNE** *drinks.*)

DON. You never give me satisfaction.

>   (**DON** *necks his wine then belches.*)

Ten

> (**ANNE** *answers emails on her phone.*)
>
> (**DON** *watches TV.*)
>
> (**DON** *sneaks a look at* **ANNE**.)
>
> (**DON** *drinks.*)
>
> (**DON** *tentatively reaches for* **ANNE** *but before he can touch her –*)

ANNE. I'm working.

> (**DON** *withdraws his hand.*)
>
> (**ANNE** *continues with her work emails.*)
>
> (**DON** *drinks and watches TV.*)

DON. Over ten thousand now...

Eleven

(**ANNE** *and* **DON** *sit in their armchairs watching TV.*)

DON. What've you done to it?

ANNE. Nothing.

DON. Had it cut?

ANNE. Taking the piss?

DON. Looks nice.

ANNE. Mullet. Looks awful. Looks like I'm in *Duran Duran*.

DON. Think it looks nice.

ANNE. What do you want?

DON. Nothing! Just saying hair looks nice that's all.

ANNE. Right... Well... It don't. So shut up.

(**DON** *drinks.*)

DON. So you're not gonna have a look then?

ANNE. I knew it!

DON. Come on!

ANNE. I've been on laptop all day.

DON. Have a look for me.

ANNE. Look yourself.

DON. You know I can't use internet.

ANNE. You're useless.

DON. Not that useless when you want decorating doing.

ANNE. Saying you'll do it for yonks.

DON. I will.

ANNE. Five months now I been waiting.

DON. Start it tomorrow. If you have a look for me.

> *(A moment.)*

> (**ANNE** *picks up her phone, opens the internet.)*

ANNE. What's it called?

DON. How do I know?

ANNE. Government what's it?

DON. Support grant is it?

ANNE. Found it.

DON. Right then.

ANNE. What's your turnover?

DON. How am I meant to know?

ANNE. Well you need to know to work out grant.

DON. Fuck knows.

ANNE. Well find out.

DON. How?

ANNE. Call accountant.

DON. Not calling him.

ANNE. Why not?

> *(A moment.)*

DON. Late.

ANNE. Call him tomorrow.

> (**DON** *drinks.)*

DON. You know I'm shit on phone.

ANNE. Shit at everything. Why can't men have a phone call?

DON. You'll want some of the money won't you?

ANNE. Half of it.

DON. Piss off.

ANNE. Quarter.

DON. Shut up.

ANNE. How much?

DON. It's to keep my business going.

ANNE. Not a business: hobby shop. And I've kept it going for years. So how much?

(*A moment.*)

DON. You know I'll treat you.

ANNE. You always treat me.

DON. There you are then.

ANNE. Badly.

(*A moment.*)

I'm on a Teams at nine. I'll call him before then. Useless man.

DON. Least I don't have a mullet.

(*A moment.*)

ANNE. Twenty thousand now...

Twelve

*(**ANNE** and **DON** drink glasses of wine. Two empty wine bottles by each of their chairs.)*

*(From her phone, **ANNE** plays "Sweet Dreams" by the Eurythmics.)*

*(**ANNE** drunkenly sings the lyrics loudly.)*

*(**DON** drunkenly bobs his head along to the music.)*

(They both glug their glass of wine.)

*(**DON** looks at the decorated roof.)*

DON. That why you're still with me then? Decorating?

(A moment.)

*(**DON** necks his wine.)*

ANNE. No.

(A moment.)

With you 'cause of the boys. Too expensive to divorce you. And I like this house.

*(**ANNE** necks her wine.)*

DON. Been twenty-nine years.

ANNE. Twenty-nine years...

(A moment.)

I know why you're with me. 'Cause I'm a cash cow.

DON. 'Cause I love you. 'Cause I like the bickering.

(A moment.)

You daft bitch.

(*They drink.*)

(*They sit and listen to the music for a while.*)

(**DON** *looks to* **ANNE**.)

(**DON** *struggles out of the chair and to his feet.*)

(**ANNE** *watches him.*)

(*Slowly, tentatively,* **DON** *starts drunk dancing.*)

(**ANNE** *watches him.*)

(**DON** *keeps dancing, waiting for* **ANNE** *to join him.*)

(**ANNE** *drinks.*)

(**ANNE** *sits and watches* **DON** *dance to the music for some time.*)

(*As the song stops,* **DON** *stops dancing.*)

(*Silence.*)

(**DON** *slowly eases himself back into his chair.*)

(**ANNE** *watches him.*)

(**DON** *drinks.*)

Thirteen

(**ANNE** *and* **DON** *sit in their armchairs.*)

(**DON** *counts out a wad of notes into two equal piles onto the arms of his armchair.*)

(**ANNE** *drinks, watches him, waits.*)

(**DON** *counts out the notes oh so slowly.*)

(**DON** *finishes counting out the notes into two piles.*)

(**DON** *removes his wallet.*)

(**ANNE** *drinks, watches him, waits.*)

(**DON** *puts one pile of notes into his wallet.*)

(**ANNE** *drinks, watches him, waits.*)

(**DON** *picks up another pile of notes.*)

(**DON** *stares at* **ANNE** *who stares back.*)

(*Then* **DON** *puts the other pile of notes into his wallet.*)

(**ANNE** *stares at* **DON** *who stares at* **ANNE**.*)

(**DON** *pockets his wallet.*)

(**ANNE** *drinks.*)

Fourteen

(**ANNE** *and* **DON** *sit in their armchairs watching TV.*)

(**ANNE** *drinks wine.* **DON** *drinks whiskey.*)

ANNE. Knew they'd do it.

DON. No you didn't.

ANNE. I did.

(*A moment.*)

DON. I knew before you.

ANNE. I got an email.

DON. I got *Daily Mail.*

(*A moment.*)

Done it quick.

ANNE. Course they have. Twenty-five thousand people…

DON. Too quick for my liking.

ANNE. You what?

DON. Rushed it.

ANNE. Worked fast. Worked on it for months.

DON. Exactly.

ANNE. Every possible scientist in the land working on it.

(*A moment.*)

DON. Might not be safe.

ANNE. Don't be stupid. You know nothing.

(**DON** *drinks.*)

(**ANNE** *stares at* **DON** *who stares at the TV.*)

Fifteen

(**ANNE** and **DON** sit in their armchairs. They drink red wine now it's autumn.)

(**ANNE** plays music from her phone, sings alone, free in her own little world.)

(**DON** watches her.)

(**DON** drinks.)

DON. Come on.

(**ANNE** looks at **DON**.)

Let's have a dance.

ANNE. Shut up.

DON. Have a dance.

ANNE. Don't want to.

DON. We're dancing.

ANNE. We're not.

DON. I said we're dancing.

ANNE. And I said we're not.

(**DON** stares at **ANNE**.)

(**ANNE** stares at **DON**.)

(**ANNE** turns up the music and sings louder.)

(**DON** drinks.)

Sixteen

(**ANNE** *and* **DON** *sit watching TV.*)

(**ANNE** *sips her red wine.*)

(**DON** *sneaks a peak at* **ANNE**.)

(**DON** *drains his full glass of red wine.*)

Seventeen

(**ANNE** *and* **DON** *sit in their armchairs watching TV.*)

ANNE. Stop it.

DON. Come on!

ANNE. You're drunk.

DON. Am I buggery.

ANNE. And you're sixty.

DON. So what?

ANNE. So stop it.

(**DON** *drinks.*)

DON. Used to.

(**ANNE** *watches TV.*)

Every day.

ANNE. Twenty-nine years ago.

DON. Twice a day.

ANNE. In a bedsit.

DON. Our castle.

ANNE. In Skegness.

DON. Skeggy Vegas. After Chaser's. Eurythmics. "Hello gorgeous".

(**ANNE** *drinks.*)

ANNE. We were different people.

DON. We weren't.

ANNE. You were.

DON. You what?

(*A moment.*)

ANNE. We were young.

DON. Young as the woman you feel.

ANNE. Shut up.

DON. You shut up.

ANNE. You're like Sid James.

DON. Give over.

ANNE. And this woman's fifty eight.

DON. So?

ANNE. So. My body's changed.

(**ANNE** *drinks.*)

DON. Mine hasn't.

ANNE. That's the problem.

DON. Still a stud.

ANNE. With that belly? With that jowl?

(**DON** *drinks and burps.*)

Pig.

DON. Cow.

ANNE. Boar.

DON. Bitch.

ANNE. Parasite.

(*A moment.*)

DON. What you doing?

ANNE. Fanning myself.

DON. Hot and bothered?

ANNE. Hot flush and can't be bothered.

DON. Always could make you hot under the collar.

ANNE. I said stop it.

DON. Come on.

ANNE. Mean it. Not joking now.

(A moment.)

*(***DON*** *drinks.)*

Eighteen

(**ANNE** *and* **DON** *sit in their armchairs watching TV.*)

ANNE. Front line...expect I'll have to have it straight away...

DON. Told you: not safe.

ANNE. Think they'd be rolling it out if it weren't?

DON. I read it.

ANNE. In *Daily Mail*?

(*A moment.*)

DON. It's true.

ANNE. It's news.

DON. Exactly.

ANNE. News story. Stories are made up.

DON. Here she goes: Enid Blyton...

ANNE. You don't believe every story you're told do you?

DON. You what?

ANNE. 'Cause you're not stupid. You're not a little boy. Are you?

(*A moment.*)

(**DON** *drinks.*)

DON. You believe story they've told you?

ANNE. What?

DON. Magic potion'll stop all this, save us, things'll go back to normal?

(A moment.)

*(***ANNE*** drinks.)*

ANNE. That's not a story.

DON. It's a fairytale.

Nineteen

(**ANNE** and **DON** sit in their armchairs.)

(**ANNE** listens to music playing from her phone. She drunkenly sings along.)

(Drunk **DON** struggles out of his armchair.)

(**DON** starts drunk dancing badly but passionately.)

(**ANNE** watches him for some time.)

(Then **ANNE** bursts out laughing at him.)

(**DON** stares at **ANNE** who stares back.)

(And **DON** grabs her hand.)

ANNE. What you doing?

(**DON** pulls at her hand.)

DON. Come on.

ANNE. Get off.

DON. Get up.

ANNE. Stop pulling me.

DON. We're having a dance.

(**ANNE** reluctantly gets to her feet.)

(**ANNE** stares at **DON** who stares back.)

(**DON** dances passionately for her.)

*(Drunk, feeling the music now, **ANNE** starts dancing enthusiastically, in her own little world.)*

*(Then **DON**'s dancing becomes more intense, sexualised, animal.)*

*(**DON** dances closer to **ANNE**.)*

*(**ANNE** tries to dance away from him but **DON** moves closer, closer, closer.)*

*(Until **ANNE** pushes him away.)*

*(And **DON** drunkenly falls down into his armchair.)*

*(**ANNE** picks up her phone, turns off the music, fast.)*

(Silence.)

*(**ANNE** stares at **DON** who stares back.)*

Twenty

(**DON** *sits in his armchair reading the* Daily Mail.)

(**ANNE** *enters with two letters from the postman.*)

(**ANNE** *hands a letter to* **DON**.)

ANNE. From the doctor.

(**DON** *takes the letter from* **ANNE**.)

Inviting us to have it.

(**DON** *stares at his letter.*)

(*Without opening the letter,* **DON** *sets it down.*)

(*As* **ANNE** *opens her letter, she stares at* **DON** *who reads his newspaper.*)

Twenty One

(**ANNE** and **DON** sit in their armchairs watching TV.)

(They drink red wine.)

DON. Must've started coming in the shop – what? – this time last year.

(**ANNE** watches TV.)

Yeah. October time.

(**ANNE** watches TV.)

About half your age she was.

(**ANNE** watches TV.)

Thin though.

(**ANNE** watches TV.)

Big bust.

(**ANNE** watches TV.)

Trying on these skirts.

(**ANNE** watches TV.)

When she just started talking about how sad she was...

(**ANNE** looks to **DON** who drinks.)

'Cause her husband...her husband won't sleep with her no more.

(A moment.)

(**ANNE** turns off the TV.)

ANNE. Come on then.

DON. What?

> (**ANNE** *drains her drink.*)

ANNE. I'm off up.

DON. Right then.

> (**DON** *drains his drink.*)

ANNE. To sleep. And don't even think about doing what you did last night.

> (*A moment.*)

DON. Don't know what you're on about.

ANNE. All over the sheets.

> (*A moment.*)

You disgust me.

> (*A moment.*)

DON. Prude.

ANNE. You what?

> (*A moment.*)

DON. If you wanted to do that next to me, I wouldn't mind.

ANNE. I'd never do that next to you.

> (*A moment.*)

See you up there.

DON. I'll be ten minutes then.

ANNE. And she's welcome to you.

Twenty Two

(**ANNE** *sits in her armchair watching TV.*)

(**DON** *sits in his armchair reading the* Daily Mail.*)*

(**DON** *looks up from his newspaper and looks to* **ANNE**.*)*

DON. How you feeling?

ANNE. Fine.

DON. Don't look fine.

ANNE. That's 'cause I'm married to you.

(*A moment.*)

Arm's just sore that's all.

DON. You look warm.

ANNE. Menopause.

(*A moment.*)

DON. Still got headache?

ANNE. Only when you talk.

(*A moment.*)

You need to get yours.

(**ANNE** *coughs.*)

(**DON** *stares at her...*)

Twenty Three

(**ANNE** *and* **DON** *sit in their armchairs and watch TV.*)

ANNE. Right. Bed.

(**DON** *turns off the TV.*)

You're in spare room.

DON. You what?

ANNE. You heard.

(*A moment.*)

DON. Not made up.

ANNE. Is now.

DON. Heater's off.

ANNE. Extra bedding on.

(*A moment.*)

DON. Don't be daft.

ANNE. I've got work. And I can't sleep.

DON. Have more to drink then.

ANNE. Can't sleep when you're like this.

(**ANNE** *drinks.*)

DON. What you on about woman?

ANNE. Don't pretend you don't know. That makes it worse.

(**ANNE** *drinks.*)

What's happened to you? Seven months, caged up, turned you into an animal? Or have you always been like this? Hid it, 'til now?

(A moment.)

DON. You wanted to.

ANNE. I wanted you to go to sleep.

(A moment.)

*(***DON*** *drinks.)*

Older you get, more you remind me of him...

(A moment.)

Dad always said you'd be like this: some...stray dog I could never tame...

(A moment.)

Twenty Four

(**DON** *sits in his armchair reading his* Daily Mail.*)*

(**ANNE** *enters with a letter from the postman and holds it out to* **DON**.)

ANNE. Another one.

(**DON** *takes the letter from* **ANNE**.*)*

You need to have it.

(**DON** *stares at the letter.*)

You're old. Overweight. Got heart condition.

(**DON** *looks at* **ANNE**, *at the letter, at his* Daily Mail, *back at* **ANNE**...*)*

(*And* **DON** *tears up the letter.*)

DON. Don't tell me what I need woman.

(**ANNE** *stares at* **DON** *who stares back.*)

Twenty Five

> (**ANNE** *and* **DON** *sit in their armchairs watching TV.*)

ANNE. You're pissed.

DON. Sober as a judge.

ANNE. Always like this on Merlot.

DON. You who's pissed.

> *(They drink.)*

ANNE. Have to be. To get in bed with you.

DON. Give over.

ANNE. Not slept for weeks.

DON. Have more to drink then.

> (**DON** *drinks.*)

ANNE. Forty thousand dead... Any other time, I'd stay at Tracey's.

DON. You what?

ANNE. Her John's high risk.

> *(A moment.)*

I'm high risk...

> *(A moment.)*

ANNE. In my own house... Where I pay the bills... I'm going nowhere.

DON. I'm not.

> *(A moment.)*

ANNE. You've got nowhere to go. No money. No friends.

DON. Got loads.

ANNE. You wonder why? I'd stay with the boys but...

>   (*A moment.*)

I don't want 'em to know. Make 'em sick.

DON. Give over woman.

ANNE. Stop calling me 'woman'.

>   (*A moment.*)

Just listen to you.

DON. You never listen to me.

ANNE. What's there to listen to?

>   (**DON** *belches.*)

All you do is belch and talk about sex.

DON. All you do is put me down and talk about yourself.

ANNE. What else is there to talk about? You don't do anything. We don't do anything.

DON. I want to.

ANNE. Sex.

DON. No.

ANNE. At your age.

DON. I'm not old. You're not.

ANNE. My body's changed.

DON. Not to me. You're still gorgeous.

>   (**ANNE** *drinks.*)

ANNE. Well you're not. Why do you think I'd want to sleep with you?

*(**DON** drinks.)*

Well?

DON. I'm your husband.

ANNE. And?

DON. And you're my wife.

ANNE. Your…! You want me to be the little wife who cooks, cleans –

DON. I offer.

ANNE. When?

DON. For years.

ANNE. Years!

DON. You wouldn't let me.

ANNE. You can't cook.

DON. Give over.

ANNE. But you're happy for me to be the breadwinner?

DON. It's what we agreed.

ANNE. Agreed!

DON. Or what you agreed and I went along with.

ANNE. 'Cause you wanted me to keep you.

DON. 'Cause you earned more than me. And the boys needed looking after.

ANNE. The boys are men now. But you're not.

DON. Shut up.

ANNE. You're the third child.

DON. Shut it.

ANNE. I feel like your Mum.

DON. You're nothing like her.

ANNE. How would she feel?

DON. What?

ANNE. If she were here, now?

DON. Don't you talk about –

ANNE. If she knew what you were doing?

(*A moment.*)

Do you know how degrading it is?

DON. Likewise.

ANNE. When I keep you?

DON. You don't keep me.

ANNE. When I've kept you all these years?

DON. I'm not a dog.

ANNE. Don't act like one then.

(**DON** *drinks.*)

DON. A man's got needs.

ANNE. Then sort yourself out.

DON. Told me to stop doing that.

ANNE. Stop doing it next to me.

DON. It's my bed too.

ANNE. All over the sheets like a teenager.

DON. We still are, in my head.

ANNE. You're sick in the head.

(**DON** *drinks.*)

And what about my needs?

DON. You what?

ANNE. You heard. I need support.

DON. I support you.

ANNE. How?

DON. Give over.

ANNE. How?

DON. Give over woman.

ANNE. Stop. Calling me. Woman. How do you support me?

> (**ANNE** *drinks.*)

DON. I did the house. Do the garden.

ANNE. Most husbands do that and they go to work.

DON. I work in the shop.

ANNE. Not for eight months.

DON. 'Cause of what's going on. Not my fault: no one about.

ANNE. Let's get rid of it then.

DON. No.

ANNE. 'Cause 'it's your head space'?

DON. 'Cause it'll make money again.

ANNE. Never made money.

DON. Just made six grand in two grants.

ANNE. Which you've not given me a penny of. Even though I got 'em.

DON. Accountant got 'em.

ANNE. Who called him? 'Cause you can't make a phone call? But you made me sit there, watch you count it all out, two piles, then pocket the lot in your wallet. So how do you support me?

(**ANNE** *drinks.*)

DON. I raised the boys.

ANNE. Fifteen years ago.

DON. Gave up decorating to stay home and raise our sons.

ANNE. Then when you had, you never went back to work.

(*A moment.*)

DON. I couldn't.

ANNE. Why couldn't you?

(**DON** *drinks.*)

You'd forgotten how to work?

DON. Give over.

ANNE. How to talk to people?

(*A moment.*)

But you can talk to sad women? Whose husbands won't sleep with 'em?

DON. You what?

ANNE. You heard.

DON. Nothing happened. She just talked at me. I'm used to women doing that.

ANNE. That's 'cause you have nothing to say.

(**ANNE** *drinks.*)

DON. I've supported you by...being here.

ANNE. Being here?

DON. Kids, parents, sisters. Promotions, redundancies. And I'm still here. After twenty-nine years.

ANNE. Twenty-nine years: God help me…

DON. Of being spoken to like dirt.

ANNE. You who speaks to me like dirt.

DON. It's affectionate.

ANNE. Is it?

DON. It's banter.

ANNE. It was.

> *(A moment.)*

Just being there…isn't the same as being there.

DON. And supporting me…isn't the same as supporting me.

> *(A moment.)*

ANNE. You're a kept boy.

DON. 'Cause you wanted me to be.

ANNE. I wanted you to be a man.

DON. You didn't.

ANNE. I did.

DON. You don't. 'Cause I am a man.

ANNE. A weak one. A spineless one.

DON. This is how we behave.

ANNE. Isn't it just…

DON. You wanted me to be a wife.

ANNE. You what?

DON. You heard. Someone you could control.

ANNE. That's not what a wife is.

DON. Not what a husband is either.

> *(A moment.)*

> *(**DON** drinks.)*

ANNE. They used to be the hands that held my boys. Held me when Dad died, Mum...our Tina. But now...

> *(A moment.)*

Do it again and I'll call the police. I'll tell the boys. I'll let your youngest arrest you. I'll press charges. Everyone will know what kind of man you are.

> *(They finish their drinks.)*

DON. I'm just a man.

ANNE. You're an animal.

DON. I'm just a man who still loves his wife.

> *(A moment.)*

Twenty Six

*(**ANNE** and **DON** sit in their armchairs.)*

(They drink red wine in silence.)

(An empty bottle by each of their chairs.)

Twenty Seven

> (**ANNE** *and* **DON** *sit in their armchairs watching TV. They drink mulled wine now it's winter.*)

DON. You've put fennel in it.

ANNE. You hear me?

DON. Who puts fennel in mulled wine?

ANNE. They want us to go out.

> (**DON** *watches TV.*)

All of us. Anyone who works in NHS. With no underlying condition. Fifty thousand dead and they want us to go out, all over, in winter, jabbing people.

> (**DON** *watches TV.*)

I'm the oldest one in our department.

DON. So?

ANNE. So... I'm scared...

DON. Scared of pricks?

> (*A moment.*)

You're jabbed.

ANNE. You aren't.

> (*A moment.*)

DON. I'll be fine.

ANNE. Will you? If they're sending me out, jabbing people, maybe you should...think about it?

> (*A moment.*)

DON. Thought about it long and hard: I don't want it.

ANNE. Chris, Keith – they've had theirs.

DON. Good for them. I'll have it in a year.

(A moment.)

ANNE. A year?

DON. If people don't have side effects.

ANNE. What you talking about: a year?

DON. You heard.

ANNE. Well...what if you get it before then?

DON. I'll be careful.

ANNE. Jacky was careful. It won't wait for you.

DON. Shut up I'm missing this.

ANNE. If I'm being sent out, you need to have it.

DON. I don't need to do nothing I don't want.

ANNE. There speaks a kept man.

*(**ANNE** drinks.)*

You're old.

DON. I'm not.

ANNE. Overweight.

DON. Shut up. All muscle. I'm big boned.

ANNE. Small brained.

DON. Just a bad cold.

ANNE. Sixty thousand dead.

DON. I'm still here.

ANNE. For now.

DON. When your time's up…

ANNE. Doesn't have to be up yet.

DON. All got to go some time.

ANNE. Not like this. Horrible death. Look at Jacky, Norris, Pam…

DON. Take my chance.

ANNE. What chance?

DON. You what?

ANNE. You heard. 'Cause if you get it, you've got no chance. Not at your age. In your health.

DON. Fit as a butcher's dog.

ANNE. Starts with a temperature. Clammy forehead. Then you're coughing, aching, knackered. Then the virus moves down the respiratory tract through the nose, mouth, throat. To the lungs which become inflamed. Which can lead to pneumonia. Which can choke you to death.

DON. Paper says it's just a cold.

ANNE. If you're jabbed!

DON. I'm not. Having it. Yet.

(*A moment.*)

ANNE. What about me?

DON. What about you?

(*A moment.*)

ANNE. What about the boys?

(**DON** *drinks.*)

They need a Dad.

DON. Not any more…

ANNE. What?

(*A moment.*)

DON. Got their own lives.

ANNE. Jacky's lads had their own lives. Now look at 'em. Want that for your boys?

(*A moment.*)

They're too young to lose a Dad.

DON. More likely to lose me from side effects.

ANNE. What side effects?

DON. Stop going on.

ANNE. What side effects? What you talking about?

DON. You can die from having it.

ANNE. You can't.

DON. Blood clots. Heart attacks.

ANNE. In extreme cases.

DON. Not according to paper.

ANNE. Daily bloody Mail…

DON. It's true.

ANNE. It's bollocks.

DON. This woman in Leeds…

ANNE. How old was she?

(*A moment.*)

How old was she?

DON. Blood clot went to her heart, killed her.

ANNE. Listen to me –

DON. They're dangerous.

ANNE. Told you: think we'd be allowed to roll 'em out if they were?

DON. Not been tested properly. Don't know what's in 'em.

ANNE. Don't know what's in paracetamol. Don't know what's in your wine.

DON. Fennel...

ANNE. Don!

(*A moment.*)

DON. I've got heart condition.

ANNE. You don't have a heart.

DON. Serious heart condition.

ANNE. Which is why you should have it. And it's not serious.

DON. Atrial fibrillation.

ANNE. Which you're on meds for. You don't know what's in them neither. But you still take 'em everyday. So you'll be fine.

(*A moment.*)

DON. Dad – the bastard – Mum – God rest her soul – both had heart conditions. Both died of heart attacks. At my age.

(*A moment.*)

Told you: if more people aren't having heart attack from it in the next year... I'll consider it.

ANNE. You're scared of dying so won't have something that could save your life?

(A moment.)

You scared of pricks?

DON. Stop being one.

ANNE. You're having it.

DON. I never 'have it' …

ANNE. You what?

(A moment.)

Get jabbed.

DON. Get fucked.

(A moment.)

You don't control me. You don't tell me what I can do with my own body.

(A moment.)

Twenty Eight

(**DON** *sits in his armchair reading the* Daily Mail.)

DON. Sixty five thousand...

(**ANNE**, *in work clothes, puts on a face mask.*)

(**ANNE** *puts on a woolly hat and gloves.*)

(**ANNE** *puts rubber gloves over the top of her woolly gloves.*)

ANNE. See you later.

(**ANNE** *looks to* **DON** *who doesn't look up from his paper.*)

Twenty Nine

(**DON** *sits in his armchair watching TV, eating his second packet of cheese and onion crisps.*)

(**ANNE**, *recently arrived home, takes off her mask and bins it.*)

(**ANNE** *takes off her rubber gloves and bins them.*)

(**ANNE** *anti-bacs her hands with a pocket hand sanitiser.*)

(**ANNE** *checks her used lateral flow test resting on the arm of her chair.*)

ANNE. Merry fucking Christmas...

(**DON** *and* **ANNE** *look at each other.*)

Thirty

*(**ANNE** and **DON** sit in their armchairs watching TV, each drinking a glass of mulled wine.)*

(But they're both wearing masks.)

(And their chairs are now two meters apart.)

*(**ANNE** lowers her mask to take a glug of wine then replaces the mask.)*

(They continue watching TV.)

*(Then **DON** coughs lightly.)*

Thirty One

(**ANNE** *and* **DON**, *in their masks, sit in their armchairs, still two meters apart.*)

(**DON** *coughs violently.*)

ANNE. You need to do a test.

DON. I'm fine.

ANNE. Don't sound fine.

DON. I said I'm fine woman. Not sticking nothing down my throat.

(**DON** *removes his mask to drink.*)

(**DON** *coughs again.*)

(**ANNE** *watches* **DON**.)

Thirty Two

(**ANNE** and **DON**, in their masks, sit in their armchairs, still two meters apart.)

DON. I knew you'd give me this.

(**ANNE** stares at **DON**.)

ANNE. Boys probably give it you. Christmas, New Year Eve.

DON. That's it: blame kids.

ANNE. Or you got it in village shop. Buying your *Daily Mail*.

(A moment.)

This is your fault.

DON. It's your fault. Going out jabbing.

ANNE. It's my job.

(**DON** coughs.)

And you should've been jabbed.

DON. I'll be fine.

ANNE. You're sweating.

DON. It's menopause.

(**DON** coughs.)

ANNE. Sixty seven thousand...

Thirty Three

(**ANNE** and **DON**, *in their masks, sit in their armchairs, still two meters apart.*)

ANNE. You should phone doctor.

DON. Don't need no doctor.

ANNE. Stop being such a man.

DON. Stop being such a girl.

ANNE. You might need hospital.

DON. It's snowing.

ANNE. So?

DON. So ambulance would never get here.

ANNE. I'll drive you.

DON. God help me.

ANNE. Do you think you need to go? To hospital?

(*A moment.*)

DON. It'll be packed.

ANNE. 'Cause… I think you need to go…

(*A moment.*)

DON. I'll catch flu, pneumonia…

ANNE. Jacky, Norris, Pam: I've seen how this starts…

(*A moment.*)

DON. I'd never come out.

ANNE. I'll get car keys.

DON. Sit. Down. I don't need no hospital.

ANNE. Don. Love. You do.

DON. Stop telling me what to do woman. You're not the boss of me.

ANNE. Don. Please. Seventy-thousand people –

DON. I said. I'm not. Fucking. Going.

Thirty Four

(**ANNE** and **DON**, *in their masks, sit in their armchairs, still two meters apart.*)

ANNE. Your hands...

(**DON** *looks at his hands.*)

ANNE. They're blue...

DON. I'm cold.

ANNE. I'm phoning 'em.

DON. You aren't.

ANNE. Should've phoned 'em days ago.

DON. I said you're not fucking phoning 'em.

(**ANNE** *stares at* **DON** *who coughs.*)

ANNE. Listen to me...last twenty-nine years...you haven't had to make any decisions. Haven't had to face any consequences.

(*A moment.*)

What should I sacrifice for that house, that holiday? Nothing: she'll pay. What happens if I don't go in to work today? Nothing: she's the breadwinner. What can I get away with? Everything: she'll put up with me 'cause she has for thirty odd years. But now...

(*A moment.*)

You had a choice to make. You made the wrong choice 'cause you're a man. You're facing the consequences.

(*A moment.*)

Now I'm gonna do what I've always done. Make decisions for you.

DON. Don't you dare.

ANNE. I'm phoning ambulance.

    (A moment.)

DON. If I'm going... I'm going at home...

ANNE. Not in my house. I'll phone 'em.

DON. I'll never forgive you.

ANNE. You think I'll ever forgive you?

Thirty Five

(The offstage sound of **DON** *coughing upstairs.)*

*(***ANNE***, panicked, on the phone.)*

ANNE. *(On phone.)* His hands...

And his lips...

His lips are blue as well now...

I think he's hypoxic...

Tracey – my colleague – she's dropped round SATS monitor.

Oxygen's sixty six instead of hundred...

*(***ANNE*** drinks.)*

Thirty Six

(Offstage, the front door is open revealing blue flashing lights of an ambulance.)

*(The sound of two paramedics pushing a stretcher along gravel to the ambulance, loading **DON** into the back of an ambulance.)*

*(**ANNE** sits in her armchair, in her mask, shivering in her dressing gown, staring offstage at the open front door, watching all of this.)*

(Offstage the sound of ambulance doors being closed, the engine starting...)

*(And **ANNE** watches as **DON** is taken to hospital...)*

Thirty Seven

*(****ANNE****, on the phone. Instead of this being represented literally, perhaps she's speaking to Don's empty chair? To the audience? Or speaking into the void?)*

ANNE. Yep...

Yep...

Right well is there any way of knowing?

If it's... Delta or doodah? Omicron?

Right...

Right.

What are his odds?

Thirty Eight

(**ANNE** *sits in her armchair video calling*
DON *on her mobile phone.*)

DON. Nothing wrong with me.

ANNE. Don.

DON. Feel fine.

ANNE. That's steroids. Wear it.

DON. Come pick me up.

ANNE. You what?

DON. You heard.

ANNE. I can't.

DON. Then I'll get home myself.

ANNE. You won't.

DON. Discharge myself.

ANNE. You can't.

DON. Watch me.

ANNE. You're...really poorly.

DON. I'm fine.

ANNE. They've told me... you're...really poorly...

DON. What they said?

(*A moment.*)

What they said to you?

(*A moment.*)

They won't tell me nothing.

(*A moment.*)

ANNE. Listen to me: please wear that mask.

DON. It's horrible.

ANNE. I know... I know love, I'm so sorry but...it's your lungs...

DON. Nothing up with my lungs.

ANNE. Smoked for thirty years.

DON. Ten year ago.

ANNE. Damage is done. You need to wear oxygen Don.

DON. Chokes me. It hurts.

ANNE. I know... But you'll choke to death if you don't wear it. Do it for me. For the boys.

Thirty Nine

(**ANNE**, *on the phone.*)

ANNE. And it's helping him, his lungs?

Right...

So...

What next: do we...prone him?

Forty

*(**ANNE** sits in her armchair video calling weakened **DON** on her mobile phone.)*

DON. Hello gorgeous.

ANNE. Hello lovely man. How you doing?

DON. Been better...

ANNE. I know. I know.

DON. But I done three hours on my belly in the mask.

*(**ANNE** chokes up but swallows it down.)*

ANNE. Good boy...

Forty One

(**ANNE**, *on the phone.*)

ANNE. Right.

Great.

Thank you. For all you're doing.

Forty Two

(**ANNE** *sits in her armchair video calling weakened* **DON** *on her mobile phone.*)

DON. How's the boys?

ANNE. Missing you.

(*A moment.*)

I'm missing you too.

DON. Are you?

ANNE. Course I am.

(*A moment.*)

Missing the bickering.

DON. And me.

(*A moment.*)

ANNE. You've got to get better.

DON. I'll have a go.

(*A moment.*)

ANNE. Got a list of jobs for you to do.

DON. Got my own list of jobs to do first! Gotta get back in the shop.

ANNE. You will. I've checked it. It's fine.

(*A moment.*)

DON. Ta.

ANNE. And I've...applied for the third grant...

Forty Three

(**ANNE**, *on the phone.*)

ANNE. Right but...

Yesterday your colleague said he was improving so...

Right well...

What happens now?

Forty Four

> (**ANNE**, *dressing gown, just woke up, answers her phone, fast.*)

ANNE. Don?

DON. Hello?

ANNE. Three o'clock in the morning. Everything alright?

DON. They told me to ring.

ANNE. Why? What's happened? What's up?

DON. They're doing it.

> (*A moment.*)

ANNE. Right... well... you'll be fine...

DON. Will I?

> (*A moment.*)

ANNE. They're just doing it to...to give your lungs a rest...

DON. Okay.

ANNE. So they can get better. Then you can come home.

DON. Hope so.

> (*A moment.*)

I better go.

> (*A moment.*)

ANNE. This isn't goodbye. It's goodnight.

> (*A moment.*)

DON. Night then.

ANNE. Night love...

(Perhaps they stay on the line breathing together for some time until Don's line goes dead.)

Forty Five

(**ANNE**, *on her phone.*)

ANNE. Hello?

It's Anne.

Don's wife...

I'm just...phoning to check how he is?

Yeah, course: my password is caged bird sixty four.

Forty Six

(**ANNE**, *on her phone.*)

ANNE. Hello. Me again. Caged bird sixty four.

Forty Seven

*(***ANNE***, on her phone.)*

ANNE. C – A – G – E – D – B – I – R – D

Forty Eight

*(**ANNE**, on her phone.)*

ANNE. Right and he's still on ninety percent oxygen?

Forty Nine

(**ANNE**, *on her phone.*)

ANNE. Eighty?

Great.

Well...not great but...

Fifty

(**ANNE**, *on her phone.*)

ANNE. Back up to ninety?

Right...

Fifty One

*(**ANNE**, on her phone.)*

ANNE. Seventy?

Fifty Two

(**ANNE**, *on her phone.*)

ANNE. Great well if he's at sixty...

Does that mean we can trache?

Fifty Three

(**ANNE**, *on her phone.*)

ANNE. Mm mm.

Mm mm.

Right so...

Where's the infection?

Fifty Four

(**ANNE**, *on her phone.*)

ANNE. Ninety again?

And are the antibiotics not...?

Fifty Five

(**ANNE**, *on her phone.*)

ANNE. Right well, ninety-five percent oxygen means…

What exactly?

Fifty Six

> (**ANNE**, *on her phone.*)

ANNE. Mm mm.

Mm mm.

Right well, been in ten days now, so...

He's no longer infectious...

Yep so does that mean I can...

Right well I can phone Tracey: she can get me there in the hour.

Fifty Seven

(**ANNE**, *in a woolly hat, scarf and gloves, just back from visiting Don in hospital, sits in her armchair.*)

(*Trying to fight back tears at what she's seen in there.*)

(**ANNE** *pours herself a drink of gin.*)

(**ANNE** *necks it and winces.*)

(**ANNE** *pours herself another.*)

(*Thinking,* **ANNE** *drinks slowly.*)

Fifty Eight

(**ANNE**, *on her phone.*)

ANNE. With respect doctor, you've seen him, I've seen him now and...

No, I know there's just one system failure but it's been two weeks and there's no...

I get that, no I get that, if there's a chance...

You can't stop treating or else you're guilty of...

But the longer he stays on there, the more chance of...

I know, I know...

But I work there too.

So, I know how it works: keep the body alive at all costs, never mind what the person inside would want.

Well, I know Don.

We've been together twenty-nine years, and we've always said: anything like this happens to us, we want the other one...

He wouldn't want to be a...

To be vegetative doctor.

And I work full time.

Mother of two. House to pay for. I can't be his carer.

I won't be.

I've been his carer for twenty-nine years so...

And he's brought all this on himself.

He's not killing me too.

Fifty Nine

(**ANNE**, *on her phone.*)

ANNE. Are you...are you with him now?

Can he...hear anything?

Right, then could you...

Could you hold the phone to his ear?

Count to ten and I'll try and...

Thank you.

...

Don?

Hello lovely man.

It's me.

If you can hear me...

Me and the boys...we're so...

Keep fighting.

We'll see you when you get out.

They love you.

I ...

I want you to know...

How you've behaved...

I ...

Hello?

Right. Oh. Okay.

Thanks Tom, no I said everything I ...

Sixty

(**ANNE**, *on her phone.*)

ANNE. What am I saying?

I'm saying you've been treating him for three weeks now and...

I know I know, one system failure, blah blah blah, but the longer he stays on there...

Brain damage, muscle atrophy...

And he's getting infection after infection...

I'm saying – God am I really saying this? – I'm saying...

Perhaps now's the time to maybe...

Stop...the antibiotics...?

Sixty One

*(**ANNE**, on her phone.)*

ANNE. Right.

Right...

Okay well I'll...

Phone his boys...

Sixty Two

(Anne and Don's empty armchairs.)

(Offstage sound of a front door opening, closing.)

*(**ANNE** enters, alone, in a woolly hat, scarf and gloves, she slowly sits in her armchair.)*

*(**ANNE** covers her face with her hands.)*

Sixty Three

*(**ANNE** sits alone in her armchair, staring at Don's empty armchair.)*

Sixty Four

(**ANNE** *sits alone in her armchair, staring at Don's empty armchair.*)

(*A glass of gin in her hand.*)

Sixty Five

*(**ANNE** sits alone in her armchair, staring at Don's empty armchair.)*

*(**ANNE** drains a third glass of gin and pours another.)*

Sixty Six

> (**ANNE**, *just out the bath, in a dressing gown, hair in a towel, sits in her armchair, on the phone.*)

ANNE. To...register a death...

Don. Don Blankley.

Yes he's my...

I'm his...

Widow...

> (*With her spare hand,* **ANNE** *feels down her armchair for the remote control...*)

Twenty-five three sixty two.

Ashton-Under-Lyne Manchester.

> (*...and* **ANNE** *finds a coin...*)

Yes that was it...

And the secondary cause was lung failure.

> (**ANNE** *stares at the coin...*)

Mm mm.

Mm mm.

Right and how much does the death certificate cost?

> (*And* **ANNE** *tosses the coin.*)

Sixty Seven

(**ANNE** *sits in her armchair eating dinner alone in front of the TV.*)

(**ANNE** *stares at the gammon and pineapple left on her plate.*)

(**ANNE** *tries to eat.*)

(**ANNE** *can't eat.*)

Sixty Eight

(**ANNE** *sits in her armchair, watching TV, binge eating cheese and onion crisps.*)

(*The sound of the* Emmerdale *theme.*)

(**ANNE** *turns off the TV.*)

Sixty Nine

(**ANNE** *sits in her armchair drinking a glass of gin. An empty bottle of it by her feet.*)

(**ANNE** *listens to "Sweet Dreams" by the Eurythmics playing from her phone.*)

(**ANNE** *opens her mouth to sing along.*)

(But **ANNE** *can't bring herself to sing.*)

(**ANNE** *turns off the music.*)

Seventy

(**ANNE** *enters carrying a tin of Dulux Goose Down paint.*)

(**ANNE** *takes in the living room that needs painting.*)

Seventy One

(**ANNE** *enters from the garden wearing Don's gardening gloves.*)

(**ANNE** *sits down in her armchair.*)

(**ANNE** *slowly takes off Don's gardening gloves.*)

(**ANNE** *holds Don's gardening gloves in her hands.*)

(**ANNE** *stares at Don's gardening gloves lying in her hands for some time.*)

Seventy Two

(**ANNE** *sorts through cardboard boxes of vintage stock from Don's emptied and sold vintage shop.*)

Seventy Three

(A pile of Don's clothes in his armchair.)

*(One by one, **ANNE** throws items of Don's clothing into a bin bag.)*

*(Until **ANNE** stops at a shirt Don's had since they first met.)*

*(**ANNE** sets down the bin bag.)*

*(**ANNE** holds up the shirt.)*

*(**ANNE** stares at the shirt.)*

*(**ANNE** smells the shirt.)*

*(**ANNE** holds the shirt to her chest.)*

*(**ANNE** sways with the shirt, as if dancing with it.)*

Seventy Four

*(**ANNE** sits in Don's armchair watching TV, drinking a glass of gin, on the phone to Tracey.)*

ANNE. No I'm back at work...

Letting me do it from home, taken me off vaccinations so...

The boys?

The boys are coping...

Luke's back on the beat, Jim's thrown himself into writing so...

Yeah... I'm pootling along...

No Tracey don't be daft you don't need to do anything.

Well...if you really want to...why don't we go out?

Dinner?

Or...dancing?

Seventy Five

("Love Is A Stranger" by the Eurythmics is playing from Anne's phone.)

*(Sat in Don's armchair, **ANNE** hums along as she applies lipstick.)*

Seventy Six

(**ANNE**, *make-up on, sits in Don's armchair, waiting to be picked up for a night out.*)

(*A moment.*)

(**ANNE** *stands up.*)

(**ANNE** *makes her way to a window.*)

(**ANNE** *looks out the window for some time.*)

(**ANNE** *opens the window.*)

(*The smell of fresh air.*)

(*The sound of life outside.*)

(**ANNE** *breathes in.*)

(**ANNE** *breathes out.*)

(*Blackout.*)

End of Play